Simply Value Us

Meeting the Needs of Young Minority Ethnic Anglicans
Committee for Minority Ethnic Anglican Concerns (CMEAC)
Youth Research Project

Church House Publishing
Church House
Great Smith Street
London
SW1P 3NZ

ISBN 0 7151 3839 1

Published 2000 for the Committee for Minority Ethnic Anglican Concerns of the Church of England by Church House Publishing.

Copyright © The Archbishops' Council 2000

All rights reserved. No part of this publication may be reproduced or stored or transmitted by any means or in any form, electronic or mechanical, including photocopying, recording, or any information storage and retrieval system without written permission which should be sought from the Copyright and Contracts Administrator, The Archbishops' Council, Church of England, Church House, Great Smith Street, London SW1P 3NZ. (Tel: 020 7898 1557; Fax: 020 7898 1449; Email: copyright@c-of-e.org.uk).

This report has only the authority of the Committee that produced it.

Front cover: *The stone carved head is part of a quire screen, built in the thirteenth century. It was placed in the 'Morning Chapel' of Salisbury Cathedral in 1790. Among the carved angels carrying symbols of the Eucharist and musical instruments are carved heads of the stonemasons who built the Cathedral. The head shown is considered by some to be that of an African, possibly a craftsman, and is seen as evidence that people from other countries were active in the Church and part of English life in the thirteenth century.*

These images have been chosen for the cover of this report to highlight the fact that there is a long history of minority ethnic involvement in the life of the Church in England. They are reproduced by kind permission of the Dean and Chapter of Salisbury Cathedral.

Cover design by Julian Smith
Printed in England by Halstan & Co. Ltd

Contents

	Foreword	v
1	**Introduction**	1
	Background to the report	1
	Survey methods used	1
	Results of written survey	1
	Summary of work with dioceses	2
	Summary of work with youth officers/workers/leaders	4
2	**Background to the research**	6
3	**Methodology**	8
	Survey methods	8
	Method of data analysis	11
4	**Research findings**	12
	Summary of the group survey findings	12
	Respondents' awareness of minority ethnic communities resident in their area	14
	Issues which the Church of England needs to address in order to meet the needs of young minority ethnic Anglicans	15
	Projects identified by the respondents	18
	Group work	19
	Importance of church denomination to young people	21
	Factors that motivated young people's participation in church activities	22
	Young people's feelings about their involvement in Church activities	24
	Involvement in cultural groups outside the Church	27

Contents

	Influence of cultural background on involvement in Church activities	27
	Issues faced by minority ethnic young Christians in the United Kingdom	28
	Young people's feelings about other Christians	29
	Young people's feelings about people from other faiths	31
	Suggestions for changes that the Church could make to encourage the participation of young people from minority ethnic Anglicans	32
	Discussions with group leaders/agencies	35
	Ways in which different cultural backgrounds of the groups may influence the nature of a group	39
	Youth leaders' views of young people's perceptions of church activities	40
	Youth leaders' views about changes which need to be made in order to encourage involvement of young people from minority ethnic groups	40
	Discussions with representatives and groups of other faiths	44
	Suggestions made by CMEAC diocesan network in response to the draft findings of the survey	47
5	**Examples of 'best practice'**	49
6	**Recommendations**	62
	References	68
	Index	69

Foreword

In April 1998 I was inducted as the Vicar of the United Benefice of the Holy Trinity with St Philip, Dalston and All Saints, Haggerston. As I reflect on how I came to take on that role, I remember quite clearly that two things stood out. First, the diversity of the community and second, the young people whom I met on the day of my interview. These were the two factors which made the difference. I knew, there and then, that this was the right place to be.

In 1999, we were reminded by the Stephen Lawrence Inquiry Report that institutional racism is alive in Britain. Although the repercussions of these findings were felt throughout the country, the greatest impact of all has been felt by the young minority ethnic population. They are the ones who continually find themselves pushed to the fringes of society. Sadly, the Church of England as an institution is not exempt from marginalizing its minority ethnic members.

This minority ethnic Youth Research Project comes at a time when the Church of England is forced, just like society as a whole, to re-examine how we enable people from a minority ethnic background to 'feel' a sense of belonging – a belonging that will see them engaged confidently with the church and the community.

Simply Value Us highlights a number of issues that the Church of England must address if it is to meet the needs of young people from minority ethnic backgrounds. Just to mention two of these issues: racism within the Church; and encouraging minority ethnic 'inclusion' within the Church. These should not just be left to the individual church leaders' 'good intentions'. A national policy of inclusiveness is needed, whereby the gifts that our young people bring are received by the Church.

I am excited by the timely appearance of this report. On the one hand, while it is true to say that it reflects some of the general findings which were stated in the Board of Education's report, *Youth A Part: Young People and the Church*, it is also true that it offers a particular view from a distinctively minority ethnic perspective. My sincere hope is that the findings will be taken seriously (especially by all those who work in multi-ethnic communities). The Church of England must not only grasp the

Foreword

opportunity of reaching out to all its young people; I believe that the Church must also become a more hospitable place so that minority ethnic youth will not only feel 'A part' but will themselves bring others in.

Acknowledgements

Sincere thanks must be given for the foresight of the Development Fund of the Church Urban Fund in providing the money to conduct this research project. With their help also, a conference will be held during which the report will be launched.

I would also like to thank Mrs Cynthia Poonam Knight for the major role she played in conducting this research; CMEAC management group (Mr Peter Ball, National Youth Officer; Mrs Doreen Finneron, CUF's National Development Officer; Mrs Glynne Gordon-Carter, CMEAC's Secretary; Miss Josile Munro, CMEAC's Youth sub-committee member); the Board of Education for its invaluable assistance through Mr Peter Ball, its Youth Officer; and also to Mrs Glynne Gordon-Carter and her team who have made the end product a reality.

Grateful thanks must also go to the young people from various dioceses, the youth leaders, the diocesan partners and the staff of Salisbury Cathedral.

The Revd Rose Hudson-Wilkin
Chair, Committee for Minority Ethnic Anglican Concerns

February 2000

CHAPTER 1

Introduction

Background to the report

This report describes the results of research commissioned by the Committee for Minority Ethnic Anglican Concerns (CMEAC) to assess the needs of young Anglicans from minority ethnic communities. The report also gives examples of good practice in relation to work with young Christians from minority ethnic backgrounds within the Church in general but mainly in the Church of England. The project work was carried out between May 1999 and January 2000.

The aims of the project were:

- to explore ways in which the Church of England is currently meeting the needs of young people from minority ethnic groups, both within the Church and in the wider community;
- to create a portfolio of examples of 'best practice';
- to identify unmet needs and suggest ways of developing the Church of England's work to meet the needs of young minority ethnic Anglicans.

Survey methods used

Two survey methods were used in the project. A postal survey was used to gain a general overview of the experiences and views of diocesan workers and partners. A semi-structured discussion process was used to gain a more detailed understanding of the views of groups of young people from minority ethnic backgrounds, youth leaders/workers and representatives of agencies.

Results of written survey

In total, 161 survey forms were sent to youth officers, CMEAC links, diocesan links, JOYNT Hope (the diocesan youth network) contacts,

Introduction

General Synod members, Church Urban Fund projects, etc., and 51 forms were returned. The issues raised by the respondents were grouped into the following broad categories:

- encourage learning about minority ethnic communities, at every level within the Church;
- help the Church to address issues of racism that exist within its structures;
- develop an ethos that values, welcomes and encourages the inclusion of minority ethnic people in the Church;
- help the Church to develop appropriate forms of organization and structures.

Summary of work with dioceses

The CMEAC management group selected nine dioceses for involvement in the project: Birmingham, Blackburn, Durham, Exeter, Gloucester, Leicester, London, Southwark and Wakefield. During the project the work with young people was carried out in: London (East, South, North and Central), Birmingham, Sheffield, Taunton, Slough and Oxford.

Seventy-eight young people in ten different groups participated in the project. The groups were made up mainly of people of African-Caribbean, Indian, Pakistani, Chinese and African origins, aged between 12 and 30. They came from Anglican, Roman Catholic, Free Church, Methodist and Pentecostal Church backgrounds.

Discussions were also held with young people and representatives of other faith groups, including the Hindu, Muslim and Sikh faiths.

The key issues raised by the young people were:

- denomination does not matter as long as it is not a set or fixed ceremonial type of service and the church is welcoming;

  motivating factors include:
  - having a space that is safe;
  - being included in planning and organization;
  - worship;

- the sense of being part of a group;
- following a habit;
- learning.

Other cultural influences on their involvement in activities included being able to meet with friends from the same background, and the influence of parents.

Several young people commented on the issues that minority ethnic young Christians face in the United Kingdom, such as marginalization: bullying in primary schools, racist remarks by friends; racist remarks by teachers; and the feeling of being unsure about their own personal identity.

How do young people feel about other Christians? Their comments were as follows:

- The Church is divided and not interested in minority ethnic groups.
- Compared to other faith groups, Christians are less united. Other church denominations have different perceptions of Christianity.
- Being part of the Church can be isolating.
- It is good to be part of a wider Church.

What are the issues which the Church of England needs to address in order to meet the needs of young minority ethnic Anglicans? The Church should:

- develop structures and skills which support young people;
- increase the range of activities which the Church offers young people, including minority ethnic Christians;
- help young people to develop a sense of responsibility and belonging;
- promote awareness of the Church among young people;
- improve the quality of services, particularly singing;
- address the problem that *'When youth is out, the Church wants them in the Church but when they are in, the Church does not know what to do with them.'*

Introduction

Summary of work with youth officers/workers/leaders

Altogether, 15 youth officers/workers/leaders from London, Birmingham, Taunton, Oxford and Stepney participated in the project. The factors which the participants felt made activities for young people successful were identified as follows:

- inclusion;
- responsiveness on the part of the leaders/workers;
- motivation as part of the activities;
- trust in the youth leader;
- flexibility in the activities;
- variety of activities;
- involvement in planning and organization;
- social events.

Therefore the issues which the Church of England needs to address in order to meet the needs of young minority ethnic Anglicans are:

- Ensure that worship and other church initiatives are relevant to the needs of young people.
- Actively promote the Church as an example of good practice in multicultural relations.
- Develop church structures that involve young people.
- Develop recognition that the existing church structure can be inappropriate and can be racist and be prepared to change it.
- Encourage openness to change.
- Be open to valuing diversity.

Examples of good practice identified during the project included:

- Act One, summer camp and leadership training, Birmingham;
- African and Caribbean Evangelical Alliance (ACEA), working with Black Majority Churches, London;
- Asian Fellowship, Sheffield;

Summary of work with youth officers/workers/leaders

- Catholic Association for Racial Justice, London;
- Aston Community Youth Project, Birmingham;
- Bible Study group, bringing Asian and English community together, Oxford;
- Black Forum and young people's visit to link churches in Zimbabwe, Southwark Diocese;
- Black Methodist Youth Conference, Methodist Church;
- Bourn Parish, support links with Congolese Refugees Church in London and Cambridgeshire;
- Chinese Fellowship, London;
- Youth Exchange Visit Programme, Chelmsford Diocese;
- Youth Forum, empowering scheme for sixth form young minority ethnic Christians.

CHAPTER 2

Background to the research

> All young people have a major contribution to make in the future well-being of our diverse multi-cultural society. As a nation, we must nurture, develop and unlock their social and economic potential, and engage their energy in building a just and fair society for themselves and for everyone else.
>
> (Sir Herman Ouseley, Preface, *Young and Equal,* 1995)

> I feel that the church must recognize discrimination in its many forms whether it is racial, cultural, sexual or religious based. Also to face it head on and to recognize the problem this can bring about. The church has to show that discrimination of any kind is unacceptable and totally un-Christlike.
>
> (Susan Bruno, young person, Diocese of Chelmsford, quoted in *Youth A Part: Young People and the Church*)

In 1992, the former Committee for Black Anglican Concerns held its first meeting with a number of young people nominated by diocesan bishops. The meeting was convened for three main reasons:

- to make contact with people under 35 years of age, as the Committee felt that Black Anglicans needed to be affirmed and encouraged to remain with and contribute to the Church of England;
- to have a discussion with younger people in order to ensure that they would be heard and their concerns addressed at the 1994 Black Anglican Celebration for the Decade of Evangelism;
- to attract many young people to the Celebration as a sign that they were being taken seriously.

Background to the research

The Celebration was outstanding for many reasons, one of which was the impressive attendance by young participants (over 70 attended), who came as members of diocesan delegations; their involvement as delegates, as presenters, as facilitators in all activities was very positive. Bishop Colin Buchanan remarked in his reflections on the workshops: *'I was also very struck by the relative youthfulness of so many of our Black participants. They were giving us the truth the way it is, and generally without hesitation.'*

In 1994, the Committee's survey report on Black Anglican membership of the Church of England in the 1990s, entitled *How We Stand*, identified the fact that Black Anglicans bring a higher proportion of children to church. Nationally there are 10 children for every 41 adults in church on a Sunday. Among Black worshippers, the ratio is 10 children to 16 adults. Between childhood and young adulthood their attendance drops.

The Committee's Youth Issues Sub-Committee, chaired by Ms Smitha Prasadam, devotes a great deal of time to confidence building and empowerment through training, and to encouraging young people to attend local, regional, national and international conferences. JOYNT Hope, the diocesan youth network, is growing. From 1998 to 1999, CMEAC was fortunate in obtaining the assistance of Ms Anne-Marie Parker, who enthusiastically committed herself to develop the youth work on a voluntary basis.

In order to develop this work, the Youth Issues Sub-Committee recommended to the Committee for Minority Ethnic Anglican Concerns (redesignated in 1996) that research should be done with minority ethnic youth to identify their needs and to assist the Committee in developing a clear focus and sharper edge to its work with young people. The Committee also hoped that the recommendations from Chapter 6 would encourage a more inclusive approach to minority ethnic young people in the Church of England.

This project, and in fact all aspects of the Committee's youth work, is being done in partnership with the Board of Education through Peter Ball, the National Youth Officer. Funding for this research project has been provided by the Development Fund of the Church Urban Fund (CUF).

The Committee for Minority Ethnic Anglican Concerns was fortunate in being able to recruit Mrs Cynthia Poonam Knight to conduct the research.

Chapter 3

Methodology

Survey methods

In order to meet the aims of the project (see page 1) two methods were used for the research work. The methods were chosen to facilitate the collection of qualitative data about the participants' ideas, feelings and experiences of issues which related to the project objectives, as well as identifying examples of 'best practice' and unmet needs.

To help develop an overall understanding of the range of activities and issues faced by the Church of England and also to develop links with active projects, a postal survey with open questions was used as a starting point for the project. The survey was sent, together with an explanation of the project's aims and objectives, to 161 contacts in different dioceses, selected by the CMEAC management group.

The main contact groups included:

- CMEAC Diocesan Link Persons and JOYNT Hope members;
- Diocesan Youth Officers/youth workers;
- members of the Committee for Minority Ethnic Anglican Concerns;
- minority ethnic members of General Synod;
- Church Urban Fund projects.

The survey covered the following key issues:

- respondents' awareness of the main minority ethnic communities living in their area of work;
- respondents' views on the main issues that the Church of England needs to address in order to meet the needs of young Anglicans from minority ethnic groups;

- identification of any projects run by the Church or related organizations in their area for young Christians from minority ethnic communities.

In order to develop a clear understanding of the issues faced by individuals, communities and organizations, a more detailed survey was carried out. This involved the use of a semi-structured interview process, based on discussions with the participant groups and using a standard open question framework developed for the survey. The discussion framework used for groups covered the following material:

- ways in which young people are involved in church;
- factors that motivate young people to participate in activities;
- young people's feelings about their involvement in church activities;
- how different cultural backgrounds influence the nature of the groups;
- issues faced by minority ethnic young Christians in the United Kingdom;
- young people's feelings about other Christians and people from other faiths;
- changes the Church of England needs to make in order to encourage young people from minority ethnic groups to participate in the Church, and to address young people's unmet needs.

This method was selected because of its capacity to encourage participants to explore and express their own ideas and experiences.

Nine dioceses with significant numbers of minority ethnic communities were selected by CMEAC for involvement in the survey. Initial contact with groups was made by writing to the Youth Officer in each diocese. If the Youth Officer was not able to identify any groups, other contacts provided by CMEAC were used to identify work with minority ethnic groups in the area.

Discussions with young people

Follow-up telephone discussions were used to explain the aim of the research to clarify any questions relating to the project and to discuss the

Methodology

possibility of meeting young people from minority ethnic communities. Subsequent discussions with groups were mostly held at meetings or events in which the young people were already involved, e.g. summer camps, black forum meetings, youth groups, Bible study meetings, Christian fellowship meetings. A small number of groups were arranged specifically for the project.

Inclusion of other faith groups

For comparative purposes and in order to gain an understanding of ways in which other faith groups addressed the needs of their young people, the survey was extended to include one Sikh group, one Hindu group and one Muslim group. The groups were contacted through their religious institutions and voluntary organizations. The same format of discussion was used with the young people from other faith groups in relation to their religious groups.

Discussions with youth workers and leaders

Discussions with youth workers and leaders were held separately from discussions with the young people with whom they worked. A semi-structured interview technique was used with the youth leaders and workers. The framework for discussions was:

- the range of activities that the youth workers were organizing for young people from minority ethnic backgrounds;
- their objectives for running these activities;
- factors that they felt made the different activities successful;
- ways in which the different cultural backgrounds of the young people they worked with influence the nature of the groups;
- what they felt were the young people's perceptions of their own involvement in these activities;
- changes they would like to suggest which the Church of England needs to make in order to address the needs of young minority ethnic Anglicans;
- any other projects or contacts which they would like to identify.

Discussions with three group leaders from other faiths were also held using the format above.

Method of data analysis

The responses from the written survey and the semi-structured interviews/discussions were recorded and grouped into categories that reflected the range of issues raised by participants. The method of presentation used in the report shows the frequency of responses and a qualitative summary of the range of issues included in each category.

Percentages and graphs show the frequency of the issues raised by the participants in different parts of the survey. The figures indicate the emphasis placed on issues raised by the participants and should not be read as statistically significant data.

> Example: 11 per cent of the participants felt that the motivation for them to attend church activities was being able to learn something. A typical comment in this category was: *'We made our own choice to come, mainly to learn something for ourselves.'*

CHAPTER 4

Research findings

Summary of the group survey findings

A total of 51 responses were received, approximately 31 per cent of the 161 survey forms sent out. Forms were returned from the following dioceses in the Church of England, shown with numbers are shown in Table 4.1.

Diocese	Number of responses	Diocese	Number of responses
Bath + Wells	1	London	9
Birmingham	3	Newcastle	1
Bradford	2	Peterborough	1
Bristol	2	Norwich	1
Canterbury	1	Oxford	3
Chelmsford	1	Portsmouth	1
Chester	1	Ripon	1
Carlisle	2	Southwell	1
Derby	2	Truro	2
Ely	1	Wakefield	1
Exeter	1	Leicester	1
Guildford	2	Winchester	2
Hereford	1	Southwark	4
Lincoln	1	York	2

Table 4.1 *Number of responses by diocese.*

Figure 4.1 *Dioceses covered in the postal survey and location of field visits.*

Research findings

Respondents' awareness of minority ethnic communities resident in their area

The range of minority ethnic groups mentioned by respondents was extensive. The largest single category was African (15 per cent of respondents). The largest combined group of communities was Asian (38 per cent), made up of South Asian, Bangladeshi, Indian, Kenyan Asian and Pakistani communities. Other communities identified by participants included African-Caribbean, 20 per cent (4 countries), European, 11 per cent (13 countries), Chinese, 8 per cent and 'Other', 4 per cent (5 countries plus travelling people).

Only 3 per cent of the respondents were unclear about the nature of the minority ethnic groups in their area of work, giving answers such as 'Black' or 'Some ethnic minorities'.

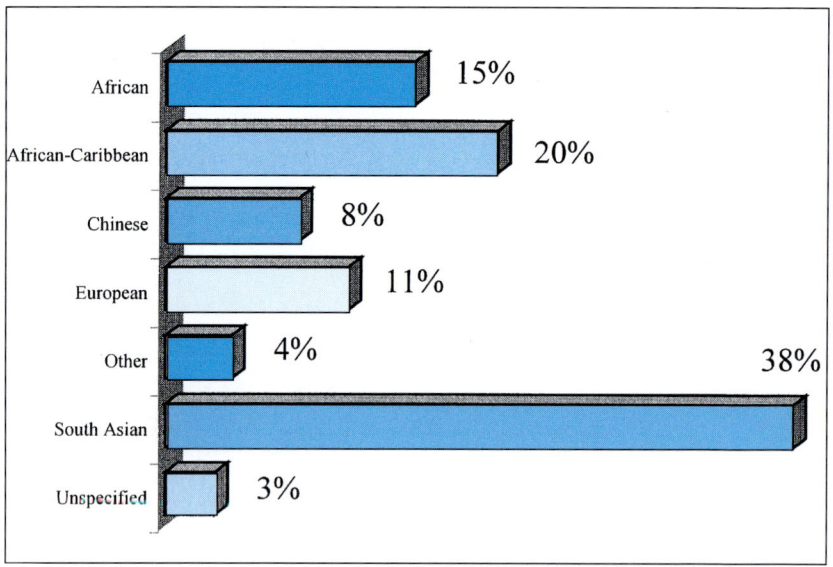

Figure 4.2 *Minority ethnic communities identified by respondents to the postal survey.*

Issues which the Church of England needs to address in order to meet the needs of young minority ethnic Anglicans

Respondents' answers fell into five main categories:

1. Encourage learning about minority ethnic people.
2. Address issues of racism within the Church.
3. Value, welcome and encourage minority ethnic inclusion in the Church.
4. Issues relating to women.
5. Issues relating to Church organization.

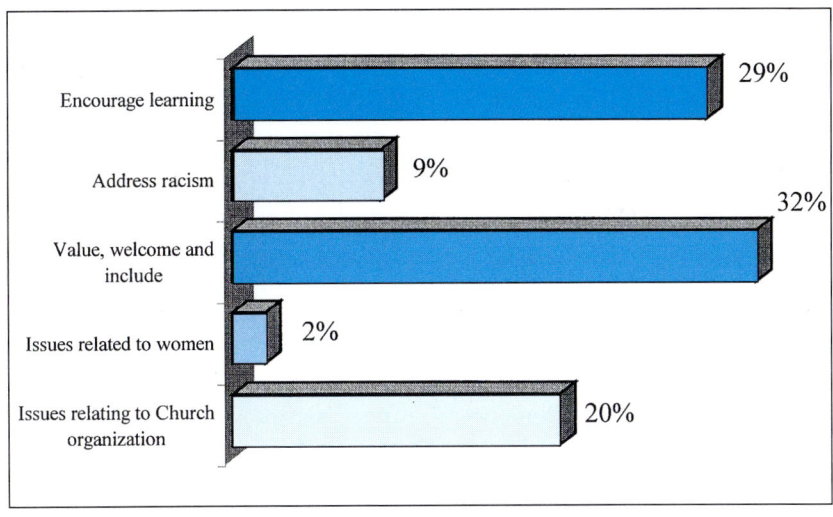

Figure 4.3 *Issues that need to be addressed by the Church of England in order to meet the needs of young minority ethnic Anglicans.*

Research findings

Encourage learning about minority ethnic people

Twenty-nine per cent of the respondents made suggestions about ways in which they felt the Church of England needed to encourage learning about other cultures and to actively raise awareness about the value of cultural diversity in order to welcome young Christians from minority ethnic communities. The need for training at different levels of the Church was also a common theme.

Examples of comments included:

> 'Sensitize the Church to the needs of marginalized communities, they should help people to deal with the prejudice they experience.'
>
> 'The Church needs to be a 'role model,' as an organization that welcomes people of all cultures and all ages.'
>
> 'Educate the Church about the existence, needs, involvement and potential of minority ethnic communities and their youth.'
>
> 'Promote awareness of cultures, cultural reverence, differences between cultures, and relationships.'
>
> 'Promote recognition and affirmation of specific cultural expressions, music, dance, traditions.'
>
> 'Help people to confront their fear of the unknown.'

Address issues of racism within the Church

Nine per cent of the respondents mentioned racism as an issue that needs to be addressed either within the Church or in the wider community. Comments included:

> 'Challenge hidden racial and cultural prejudices in the Church.'
>
> 'Tackle institutional racism: develop a strategy for dealing with racism in parishes, youth groups and schools.'
>
> 'The Church needs to help one minority ethnic community not to be racist against other minority groups.'

Issues relating to women

Only one respondent identified the need for work with women and girls from minority ethnic groups. The respondent was particularly concerned about the needs of Asian women.

Value, welcome and encourage minority ethnic inclusion in the Church

Almost one third (32 per cent) of the respondents felt that the Church needed to develop a sense of value for the spiritual and social contribution that minority ethnic Christians have made and are making to the life of the Church. Key issues identified by respondents included the need to develop the ability to listen to young people and the encouragement of active participation in Church structures. Examples of responses included:

> *'Value the young minority ethnic Christians and the mainstream youth.'*
>
> *'Communication, listen to them.'*
>
> *'Make young people welcome and take them seriously.'*
>
> *'Actively encourage young peoples's participation in Church structures at all levels.'*
>
> *'Help them to have a sense of belonging to the Church and others in the community.'*
>
> *'Make space for young people so that they can make spiritual connections to their background and identity.'*

Issues relating to Church organization

Thirty-five respondents felt that specific changes in the structure of the Church were needed to enable it to include minority ethnic Christians. The range of suggestions made in this category included: strategic planning for inclusion of minority ethnic Anglicans; allocation of financial and human resources; and development of support structures. In relation to spirituality and worship, participants suggested the following: adoption of inclusive patterns of worship; openness to music from other cultures; and

Research findings

develop ways of integrating the experience of minority ethnic Christians into the spiritual experience of the wider church. Key comments included:

> *'Provide access and support mechanisms for young people.'*
>
> *'Make it real, include minority ethnic young people in every aspect of the church, music, etc., be inclusive, not dominant.'*
>
> *'Ability to be free and flexible in worship (difficult in Church of England's attachment to fixed views).'*
>
> *'Ability to be part of an 'equal opportunities' culture, to see people as people rather than where they are from.'*
>
> *'Financial support for projects that nurture the relationship between White-led churches and Black-led churches.'*
>
> *'More pastoral care and visiting.'*
>
> *'Ensure that the church targets all young groups in their area and does not preclude their involvement.'*
>
> *'Need to have action programmes.'*
>
> *'A good social life.'*

Projects identified by the respondents

Figure 4.4 presents the frequency of the responses to the question, 'Please identify any projects, run by the church or related organizations, in your area.'

Thirty-two per cent mentioned activities like youth clubs, Bible study groups, etc., which were run for specific minority ethnic communities in their area. Fifteen per cent were aware of similar activities that were run for mixed minority ethnic communities. Thirty-seven per cent of the respondents said that they were not aware of any projects in their area which were run by the church or related organizations for minority ethnic young people. Nine per cent said there were no separate arrangements for minority ethnic young Christians in the area, so they joined in the activities run for young people in general.

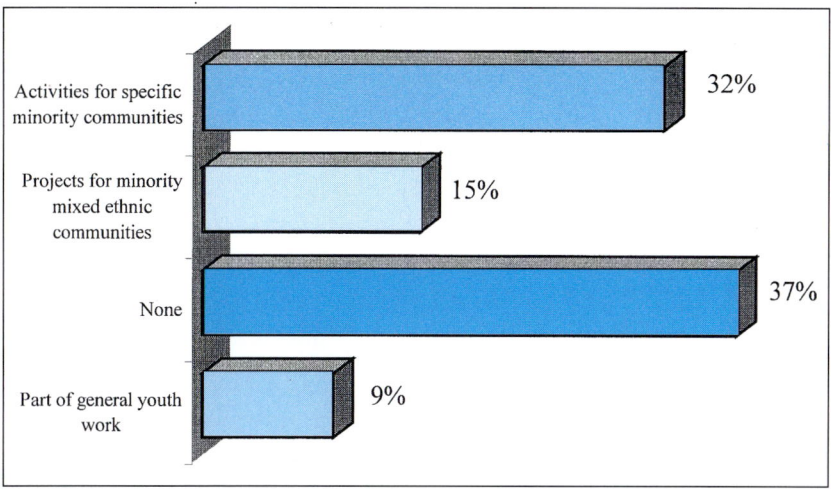

Figure 4.4 *Types of projects identified by the respondents.*

Group work

Seventy-eight young people from 10 different groups participated in the research, 38 male and 40 female, aged between 12 and 30. (Three of the participants were aged 9, 10 and 11.) Most (66) were in full-time education and 12 were working. The majority (62) were born in the United Kingdom or had come there as infants. The others (16) had lived in the UK for 2 to 15 years. Approximately 16 per cent of the young people were involved in more than one church. Approximately 40 per cent said they were regularly involved with their group.

Location of groups
- Birmingham
- North London
- Central London
- East London
- South London
- Oxford
- Sheffield
- Slough
- Taunton and Bridgwater

Research findings

CULTURAL BACKGROUND OF GROUPS AS DEFINED BY PARTICIPANTS
- Black-English
- Jamaican
- Nigerian
- Mixed race
- Chinese from Hong Kong
- Chinese from Mainland China
- Chinese, British-born
- Indian, Punjabi and Goan
- Sri Lankan
- Pakistani
- British Pakistanis

DENOMINATION OF PARTICIPANTS IN GROUPS
- Anglican   46
- Catholic   11
- Free Church   6
- Methodist   12
- Pentecostal Church 3

A summary of the range of activities in which the young people were involved is shown in Table 4.2.

Table 4.2 *Range of activities*

Activity	No.
Activity planning	11
Annual conference	19
Art work, plays	10
Barbecues	11
Basketball	6
Bible study	14
Chinese writing	6
Cinema and reflection	7
Cooking	6
Drama	17
Football	6
Fund raising	2
Helping in church	21
Occasional events	17
Sharing/fellowship	17
Singing	27
Snooker	11
Socializing	25
Summer camps	15
Teaching sessions	11
Tennis	22
Trips/outings	19
Worship	45

Importance of church denomination to young people

Most of the young people (96 per cent) felt that belonging to a specific denomination was not important; 67 per cent said that it was feeling included and whether or not their needs were met that were important; 29 per cent said that although they would be happy to attend any church, they would be put off by worship that had fixed 'ceremonial services'.

Research findings

Comments included: *'The denomination is not important, as long as its welcoming, values us and meets our needs.'*

Only 7 per cent of the respondents said they preferred going to the Anglican Church even though they would go to other denominations. A larger number, 14 per cent, said they did not really know what differences existed between different denominations.

Factors that motivated young people's participation in Church activities

The range of different factors that the young people listed as important to their participation in Church activities fell into six main categories:

1. Provision of an environment that feels safe
2. Being included in organization
3. Worship
4. Being part of a group/community
5. Habit
6. Learning.

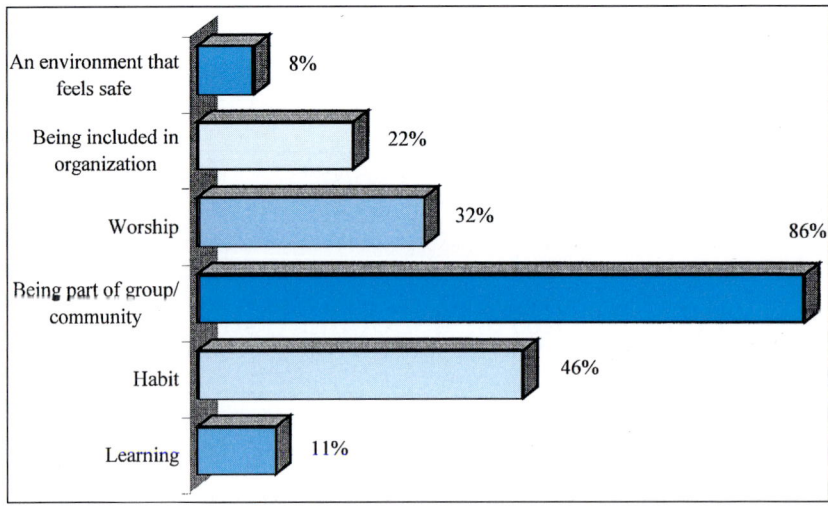

Figure 4.5 *Factors that motivate involvement of young minority ethnic people in Church activities*

Factors that motivated participation in Church activities

1. AN ENVIRONMENT THAT FEELS SAFE

For a small number of the young people (8 per cent) the feeling of being in a safe environment was an important factor in attending different activities organized by the church. The fact that church-based activities enabled them to get away from their family but with the approval of their parents was also important.

2. BEING INCLUDED IN ORGANIZATION

Being involved in the organization of activities was raised as an issue by 22 per cent of the young people. The overall impression given was that they valued both being taken seriously and the opportunity to make a difference in the Church. Involvement in planning and organization was felt to be important because it encouraged a sense of ownership which helped to maintain continued participation A further 10 per cent said that by encouraging active involvement in organized youth activities the Church helped to increase skills and encourage self-expression. A participant made the following comment at a 'Youth Forum' day that looked at racial justice issues: *'By taking part in days like this it helps us develop our skills and communicate our ideas.'*

3. WORSHIP

Approximately one-third (32 per cent) of the young people identified involvement in worship as an important part of their participation in the church. Thirteen per cent also mentioned taking communion or being able to help with the communion as special. Singing, either in a choir or just being able to sing in the service, was valued by 22 per cent. Involvement in the service – singing, praying, reading – were identified as important factors in 20 per cent of the young people's responses.

4. THE SENSE OF BEING PART OF A GROUP OR COMMUNITY

The majority (86 per cent) of the participants felt that being part of a group or community was a key reason for them wanting to be involved in services or activities run by the church. Fourteen per cent also felt that being part of the church helped them to define their sense of belonging or a sense of togetherness. Sixteen per cent talked in terms of valuing 'fellowship' with other people of their faith. Almost half (47 per cent) felt that the church enabled them to meet friends that they could not meet at other times. This was largely due to factors like being at different schools, living in different areas or working in different places. The sense of being part of a wider community, which included immediate family members like parents and grandparents, was a significant factor behind many (62 per cent) of the young people's involvement in the church.

5. Habit

Just under half (46 per cent) of the young people felt that their involvement in the Sunday activities, whether it was the service or a youth club, had become a habit. Several had attended church events on Sunday for as long as they could remember. Approximately 31 per cent made comments like: *'As the rest of the family is involved in the service we have nothing much else to do'*.

6. Learning

Eleven per cent of the participants felt that the motivation for them to attend was being able to learn something. A typical comment in this category was: *'We made our own choice to come mainly to learn something for ourselves.'*

Young people's feelings about their involvement in Church activities

It was clear from the responses of all the groups that, in addition to having to cope with the experience of young adult life, many also had to address issues that related to cultural identity. The issues appeared to arise out of the contrast between the following factors:

- the young people's cultural backgrounds;
- wider youth culture in the UK;
- their identity as Christians and young people from different faiths but from the same cultural background;
- cultural differences between themselves and their older family members.

The feelings experienced by the young people appeared to fall into five broad categories:

1. Feelings of separation from others, older family members and wider Church;
2. Valuing inclusiveness;
3. Valuing choice;
4. Dislike of pressure from Church leaders;
5. No direct participation.

1. FEELINGS OF SEPARATION FROM OTHERS, OLDER FAMILY MEMBERS AND THE WIDER CHURCH

During discussions relating to their involvement in the activities run by the Church, 43 per cent of the young people expressed the feeling of separation from others, that is, older family members, and also from the wider Church. For some (28 per cent), particularly young people from Asian and Chinese backgrounds, the sense of isolation arose because they did not understand the service fully if it was in their parents' language. Comments included: *'A lot of the time we do not understand the service if it is in our parents' language.'*

Some English-speakers (7 per cent) found the English vocabulary used by the Church difficult to understand. Consequently they found it difficult to participate in services. Thirty-two per cent, who were part of the youth activities run by the Church, said that they did not feel part of the main Church, as they were not consulted, involved or informed about the decisions made by their church.

2. FEELING INCLUDED IN THE CHURCH IS IMPORTANT

Where the participants were included in the different roles involved in running activities, they clearly appreciated the sense of value that the Church gave them; 10 per cent of the participants also reported that they were part of planning and organizing activities; 22 per cent made comments that emphasized the importance of being part of the life of the church. A sense of inclusion was also important in relation to worship: *'Worshipping with other people makes you feel like a bigger family.'*

Research findings

3. CHOICE OF OPTIONS FOR INVOLVEMENT IS IMPORTANT

Flexibility and choice in the options for involvement were felt to be important by over half (54 per cent) of the participants; 11 per cent said that they were happy about their involvement because it was their own choice to attend the activity.

4. DISLIKE OF PRESSURE FROM CHURCH LEADERS

Although a sense of inclusion was important to participants it was also clear that the young people disliked the pressure put on them by some youth leaders and church ministers, to participate in activities run by the Church. Several of the participants (19 per cent) felt that they were asked to participate in all the Church's activities without regard being given to other commitments and interests that they might have. A typical comment was: *'Sometimes we feel too pushed to get involved, we are asked to participate in each and every event.'*

Another group raised the issue of tokenist inclusion of minority ethnic young people, just to show that there was something going on for them. The point was illustrated by a group from a minority ethnic background who were involved in singing.

> *'It really makes us feel frustrated when we are asked to go to every event and play music and sing, we do not mind doing so every now and then but it gets too much when it is at each and every occasion. It also makes us feel that we are being used to put the other minority ethnic young people down when we are introduced as young people involved in the life of church.'*
>
> *'When we sing in other churches we feel that the other young people see us as all goody goody.'*

5. FRUSTRATION AS A RESULT OF NO DIRECT PARTICIPATION

Some 14 per cent of the young people expressed feelings of being bored and frustrated with the Church, primarily due to not having any say in the planning and organizing of the activities. A slightly larger number (16 per cent) felt that the Church did not really offer anything for young people and in particular it did not recognize and value young people from minority ethnic communities. A larger number (32 per cent) felt that even though there were activities for young people, the way they were organized did not take into account the abilities and talents of young people. During a group discussion one participant commented:

> 'We never have something like this [the discussion group] in our church where we sit together with someone and talk. It would be nice to have discussions about what we like doing and what talents we have. I like drawing and writing and I would like to use it but I have never been asked to use my ideas or express myself in the Church.'

Involvement in cultural groups outside the Church

In addition to their participation in the Church, 20 per cent of the young people were involved in other cultural activities. Examples included:

- Involvement in voluntary work at the Chinese Centre;
- Community work;
- Youth clubs;
- Notting Hill Carnival;
- Museum displays of different cultures;
- Charity and fund raising;
- Gospel singing groups.

Influence of cultural background on involvement in Church activities

In discussions about feelings and experiences of ways in which cultural identity may have influenced the participants' involvement in Church-related activities, just over a quarter (26 per cent) of the participants felt that culture and language united them as a group. Examples included

Research findings

enjoyment of Punjabi/Urdu worship, being with other Chinese friends, and sharing together in the same language.

Parents were a major factor in Church involvement. Seventy per cent of the participants made comments such as *'Our parents tell us to come'*. Only a few participants (10 per cent) felt that religious role models and the church minister also influenced their culture.

Issues faced by minority ethnic young Christians in the United Kingdom

MARGINALIZATION

Nearly half (49 per cent) of the young people involved in the discussion groups identified dealing with marginalization due to their cultural background as an issue that they faced. While the groups clearly recognized that other minority ethnic groups faced similar problems, some participants also described ways in which, as Christians, they had experienced bullying by other minorities. For example, young people from Asian communities described bullying and negative questioning by other Asians as a result of them being Christian rather than Hindu or Muslim Asians. A small number (4 per cent) of the young Christians from Indian backgrounds pointed out that at school they were bullied and questioned by young people of the Hindu faith as low caste people who had converted to Christianity. Others commented: *'We get asked by young people from Indian backgrounds if we became Christians because we were a low caste in India.'*

Many (10 per cent) of the young Christians from Pakistani backgrounds made similar comments. Their experience had been that young Pakistani Muslims often assumed that they came from families who had converted to Christianity when they came to the UK or that they were 'half-caste'. Twenty per cent of all the young people had experienced bullying at different stages in school due to their skin colour or just for being different. Another 14 per cent said that they had faced racist remarks by their peers in school or in the community, 5 per cent had experienced racist remarks from their teachers at school. For some the problems had become worse as they grew older: *'At primary school I did not feel I was different but in secondary school it was strong.'*

Some of the young people felt that being part of a minority group helped them deal with racism. Nineteen per cent said that they felt secure hanging around with a group of friends who shared their language and cultural values and stood up for them. Ten per cent said that in their experience Christian young people were more polite and respectful than non-Christian young people.

LACK OF CONFIDENCE ABOUT THEIR IDENTITY

Thirty-two per cent of the young people expressed their feelings of being unsure about their identity; 22 per cent felt that their culture was different from their parents as a result of having grown up in a different, multiculture and multi-faith society. Others talked about being unsure about their identity in relation to being Asian Christians. Comments included:

> 'A lot of the time I ask the question what is my identity? I am Asian but not Muslim and Christian but not white, where do I fit in the community?'
>
> 'At times we feel left out and lonely, there are not many Asian Christian families around here, there are other Asian young people around, but a lot of the time they do not consider us Asian.'

Young people's feelings about other Christians
IT'S GOOD TO BE PART OF A WIDER CHURCH

Just over a quarter (26 per cent) of the young people made comments which related to a sense of value derived from being part of the Christian community in the United Kingdom. Comments also included feelings of safety: *'It feels good and secure to know that there are other Christians around us.'*

Research findings

THE CHURCH IS DIVIDED AND NOT INTERESTED IN PEOPLE'S IDENTITY AND CULTURE

Over a third (35 per cent) of the young people felt that the Church often seemed to be divided into many different parts and, despite claims to be interested in the issues of young people and minority ethnic communities, in reality it is not interested at all. Ten per cent of the young people felt that mainstream Christians did not really care about their own faith.

A number of young people compared their experience of church life in the UK with their experiences in the countries from which their parents had come. One person described his experience of attending church in Mauritius:

> *'There, going to church is seen as a special occasion for everyone. People made sure that they wore their best clothes and looked neat and tidy, here I have noticed people do not really care how they dress when they go to church. I am not saying one is right and the other is wrong, I know the important thing is in our hearts not what we wear, but still making going to church a special event feels nice.'*

BEING PART OF THE CHURCH CAN BE ISOLATING

Eleven per cent of the young people talked about feeling isolated and lonely at times in the Church. Others felt that the services and the singing were boring and old-fashioned. A key issue was the lack of options for involvement in different areas of the Church. They also said that they felt that having a faith is not popular in the wider community or when they are at university.

OTHER CHURCHES HAVE DIFFERENT CULTURES AND DIFFERENT PERCEPTIONS OF CHRISTIANITY

Some 23 per cent expressed their feelings about how Churches in different cultures and denominations portray Jesus and other Christian values in different ways. Comments included:

> '*I find it interesting people fighting over whether Jesus was Black or White. To me it's not important what he looked like, the important thing is what message he brought to us.*'
>
> '*In materials produced by some of the Church denominations, God is portrayed as an old man with white beard, etc. I feel by showing God in this way we actually limit God, my understanding is that as Christians we believe that our God is almighty.*'

Young people's feelings about people from other faiths

Being part of a multi-faith community is a positive thing: 10 per cent of the young people said that they find it interesting learning about other faiths and the way people practice their religion. One of the young people said:

> '*I went to stay with my friend who belongs to the Muslim faith, he was going to the mosque on Friday to say his prayers, I asked him if I should stay behind but he said no you can come too. When we got there I asked him if I will have to go into the prayer room with him, he said no you do not have to join in if you do not believe. I had to wait for him while he went for his prayers, but it all felt nice and peaceful.*'

It is essential that people of different faiths maintain mutual respect: 39 per cent of the young people who had friends or work colleagues from other religions felt that it was important as a multicultural society for people from different religions to respect each other's beliefs and values. In their experiences it worked fine, when there was mutual respect.

Each faith group keeps to itself: 50 per cent of the young people said that they had friends from other faiths but they did not really discuss their faith. Twenty per cent said that they felt that the young people from other faiths, especially the Sikh and Hindu faiths, tended to stick together more in their faith groups compared to Christian youth.

Research findings

Suggestions for changes that the Church could make to encourage the participation of young people from minority ethnic groups

Over half (58 per cent) of the participants made suggestions relating to the need for development of Church structures that recognize, acknowledge and value different cultures. Some of the comments made by young people included: *'The Church needs to acknowledge the differences of the communities it serves and learn to celebrate these differences.'*

Fifteen per cent suggested that the young people need to have role models within the Church structures to look up to, people with skills to relate to people of different ages at their level. Others emphasized the need for the Church to talk with them and work with them at their level, as well as to draw ideas and feelings out of the young people. Eleven per cent of the young people suggested that the clergy and other people who are working with young people need to get the balance right in dealing with them; not to go too over the top and not to ignore them totally. Key comments included:

> *'There is a lack of role models in the Church.'*
>
> *'They need to get the balance right without patronizing.'*
>
> *'They are either over-sensitive to the needs of young people or under-sensitive.'*

Almost one third (31 per cent) of the young people said that it was important to consider appropriate timing when planning activities. In communities where parents were running their own business, for example restaurants, take-away shops or taxi services, they were unable to drop off and collect their young children on certain days of the week. A common comment related to this was: *'Take into account the time of activity, our parents cannot bring us at certain times because of their business, some times we miss out on events that we would like to participate in due to this reason.'*

Suggestions for changes that the Church could make

IMPROVE THE QUALITY OF SERVICES, PARTICULARLY SINGING

Thirty-two per cent of the responses made by the young people were related to the quality of the worship services in the Church, especially singing. Some of the comments included:

> *'Encourage music and singing that young people like.'*
>
> *'More funds to liven up services.'*
>
> *'Lively singing and services.'*

HELP YOUNG PEOPLE TO DEVELOP A POSITIVE CHRISTIAN IDENTITY AND AWARENESS OF THE RESPONSIBILITIES INVOLVED IN BEING PART OF THE CHURCH

Some 50 per cent of the young people saw the role of the Church as helping young people to develop a sense of responsibility and belonging, by valuing them and including them in the Church as an institution. Fifty per cent of the participants also made comments about the main Church and not only in the activities for young people. The comments that appeared again and again were:

> *'Involve young people in the main church, the PCCs and other committees.'*
>
> *'Give young people a sense of belonging.'*
>
> *'Simply value them.'*

Just under a quarter (22 per cent) of the young people said that there are times when they think: 'What is the difference between us and our friends from other faiths or friends that are non-believers?' They felt that a lot of the time when they compared their own religion with that of others they did not see any difference. They wanted the Church to show, through its actions, roles and teaching, the things that are unique to Christian life.

Research findings

> 'Show and help young people experience the value of being involved in the church and what is different about being a Christian.'

INCREASE THE RANGE OF ACTIVITIES IN WHICH THE CHURCH IS INVOLVED

Nearly all (98 per cent) of the young people who took part in the project suggested that the range of activities offered by the Church needed to be increased. Some 19 per cent also felt that it was essential to invite and encourage young people to become part of the Church. Key issues were participation in church activities and involvement in shaping the life of the church. One comment in particular seemed to sum-up the participants' feelings: *'You know, when we are outside the Church they want us to be in the Church, when we are in the Church they do not know what to do with us.'*

At the same time, minority ethnic young people who attended events like 'The Time of Our Lives', arranged by the Archbishops' Millennium Youth Initiative, appreciated being invited to it and enjoyed being part of it. One comment was: *'It was nice to meet other young people and participate in the event, activities and events like this need to be advertised widely so that more people can get to know about them and join in.'*

PROMOTE AWARENESS OF THE CHURCH

Some 37 per cent of the participants felt that there was a great need within the young Christian community to learn about the role of the Church and the responsibilities of being part of it. Comments included:

> *'A lot of the times we do not understand why we do certain things, no consultation takes place with us in doing things.'*
>
> *'Raise awareness in young people of what the different denominations are.'*
>
> *'Help young people from minority ethnic groups to understand their faith and history.'*

COMMUNICATION

Slightly less than half (41 per cent) of the young people identified the need for better communication systems within the different churches for young people from minority ethnic groups. They recommended better information networks that could link the different groups working in different areas and provide information about the variety of events and activities that they were involved in. Three per cent felt that newsletters or magazines to circulate information about youth activities would be a good idea; 7 per cent suggested a system of pen friends.

Discussions with group leaders/agencies

Altogether, 15 youth leaders/youth workers (7 male and 8 female) participated in the discussions during the research. Participants included people working nationally with young people in addition to those working locally in areas such as Oxford, different parts of London, Taunton and Birmingham.

The youth workers/leaders included people from African-Caribbean, Pakistani, Indian, Punjabi, Chinese, English, Malaysian and mixed race backgrounds. All came from Christian communities, 12 attended Anglican churches while the rest attended different Free Churches. They worked with children and young people between the ages of 2 and 24, within the community, schools, youth clubs, etc. The young people they worked with came from Christian and other faith backgrounds and from different cultural backgrounds.

The main range of activities that the youth workers/leaders were involved with (see Figure 4.6) included:

1. **Community events:** community celebrations, parties and social events.

2. **Social action and group activities:** including redecorating buildings, trips to various places, drama, discussions about issues like bullying, sexual health discussion, career advice, encouraging involvement in planning activities.

3. **Youth worship and spiritual development:** assemblies, group Bible study, confirmation classes, fellowship and worship, outreach work.

Research findings

4. **Cultural development:** this included activities to help young people learn about their traditional and cultural roots, for example, a Chinese group organized sessions to help the young people learn to read and write Chinese languages, Chinese cooking, film appreciation and music.
5. **Sports:** these included, swimming sessions, bowling, indoor games, ice skating, football, etc.

Activity	Percentage
Community events	15%
Social action and group activities	23%
Spiritual development	18%
Cultural development	17%
Sports	24%

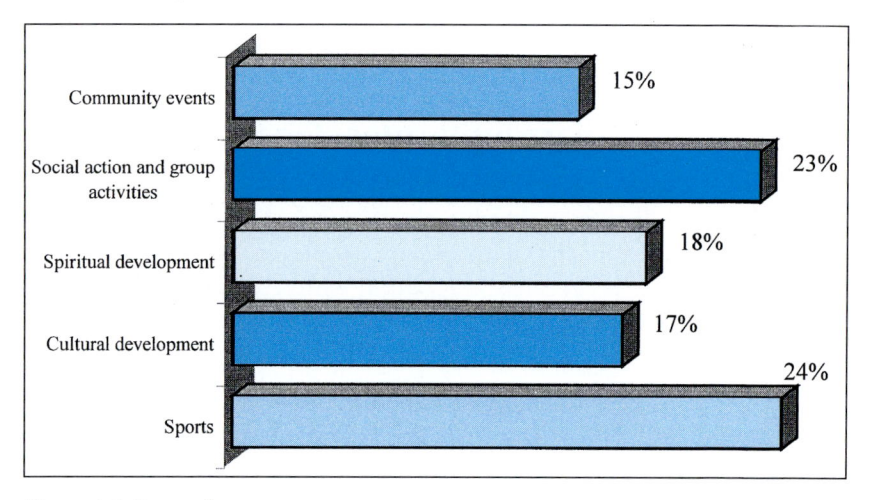

Figure 4.6 *Range of activities*

The main objectives identified by the youth workers/leaders for running youth activities fitted into four main categories:

1. **Personal and social skill development:** provide young people with an opportunity to meet others of their own age and to build relationships. Help young people build their self-confidence and self-esteem.
2. **Sharing cultures** (food, ideas, music): to help young people recognize and value specifically the cultural background of their family and to help them discuss their experience of growing up.
3. **Religious and spiritual development:** activities designed to develop an understanding of God in holistic ways, in order to encourage fellowship and shared learning about God. *'It is to help young*

people understand that our God is a God of fun'. Other activities in this category included organization of Bible study and other teaching sessions to help young people's spiritual growth. Also organizing evangelical activities, encouraging young people to share their faith with others.

4. **To provide support which values young people as themselves:** providing emotional support especially for the over-seventeens. Providing an environment where young people have freedom to feel comfortable about planning and organizing activities at their level. Activities which encourage and stimulate ideas, where their needs are responded to rather than assumptions made, as well as the provision of practical support, information and resources.

Group leaders' views of the reasons why activities were either successful or unsuccessful included seven key areas as shown in Figure 4.7:

1. Recognition of the importance of encouraging inclusive feelings
2. Responsiveness on part of the leaders
3. Trust and confidentiality
4. Motivation
5. Flexibility
6. Social events
7. Socializing.

Factor	%
Inclusion	27%
Responsiveness	15%
Trust and confidentiality	15%
Motivation	16%
Flexibility	8%
Social events	9%
Socializing	8%

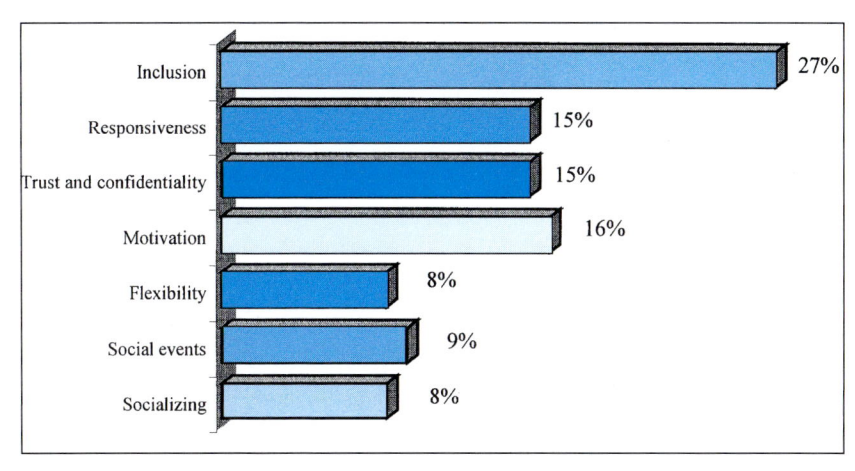

Figure 4.7 *Factors which group leaders felt made activities successful*

Research findings

1. Recognition of the importance of encouraging inclusive feelings

Most of the youth leaders felt that the biggest factor that motivated and encouraged young people to participate in various activities was whether or not they felt included by the leaders and other members of the group. Some of the comments included: *'They feel valued and included when they are involved in the planning of different activities.' 'Another big motivating factor for the young people that encourages them to participate in activities is feeling respected and valued for being who they are.'*

2. Responsiveness on the part of the leaders

The other important factor that the group leaders felt encouraged young people to join in activities is when they feel that their needs are being responded to. Some of the comments made by leaders were:

> *'It makes a lot of difference when the young people feel their suggestions are being listened to and responded to. Even if the response is negative or it is not possible to take their ideas on board immediately, they like to know what is happening.'*
>
> *'A genuine enthusiasm on the part of the leaders is very important to show that they really are interested in working with young people. Showing interest in what they are interested in.'*
>
> *'Young people value proper and clear communication. It is also important that we work with them at the level they are without assuming things, or working with them with agendas that are pre-determined by the Church.'*

3. Trust and confidentiality

Other important motivational factors identified by the group workers were trust and confidentiality.

4. Motivation

Motivation on the part both on the part of the youth leader and participants was also identified as an important factor in making an activity successful.

5. Flexibility

Flexibility in the range of activities that the individuals could participate in was also identified as one of the motivators that the youth leaders thought encouraged young people to participate. Some of the comments included: *'Freedom to choose the subjects of discussion, flexibility in the way things are planned and arranged.'*

6. Social events

Variety in the kind of activities offered was another factor that the youth leaders thought motivated youth participation. *'A variety in the activities provided, as well as activities and discussions that motivate, innovate and stimulate ideas in young minds are highly valued by young people.'*

7. Socializing

Factors which help young people socialize in a safe environment with people of their own age range were: support for sharing ideas and talents, music, food, culture, faith, building relationships and a strong partnership between church and the community.

Ways in which different cultural backgrounds of the groups may influence the nature of a group

All the group leaders felt that the cultural backgrounds of young people had an influence on the nature of the groups. Also they believed that it is very important to recognize the influence that different cultures can have on people's experiences, understanding and values. Linked to this, the youth leaders emphasized the importance of recognizing cultural diversity and being flexible in planning so that individuals and groups can maintain their identity. *'Common ways of communicating, music and values* are key factors that a lot of young people from minority background enjoy in a group situation.'

Equally commonly held was the view that parents strongly influenced minority ethnic young people in their attendance at church-related activities. 'Sometimes they like to hold to their cultural values even more strongly then their parents.'

Youth leaders' views of young people's perception of church activities

A general feeling among the youth leaders/workers was that young people up to the age of 10–11 years are happy to attend and participate in activities that are organized for them. But from then on they feel much happier if they are part of the whole process of planning and organizing activities. Comments included:

> 'Teenagers feel valued when they are consulted and involved.'
> 'Enabling young people to have a sense of responsibility and participation in church is essential.'

In addition to highlighting the positive aspects of the church's work, some participants were critical of the Church's lack of commitment to minority ethnic groups and felt that this had a negative effect on minority ethnic young people's views of the Church.

Youth leaders' views about changes which the Church of England needs to make in order to encourage involvement of young people from minority ethnic groups

In discussion about options for change that the Church could make to encourage minority ethnic young people, the following issues were raised:

Youth leaders' views about needed changes

- Actively promote the Church as an example of good practice in multicultural relations.
- Make sure worship and other church initiatives are relevant.
- Develop Church structures that ensure the involvement of young people.
- Recognize that the existing Church of England structure is inappropriate and can be racist.
- Be open to valuing diversity.

Category	Percentage
Set a good example in multicultural relations	3%
Make sure that worship is relevant	4%
Recognize that the Church of England structure can prevent inclusion	7%
Recognize that the Church of England structure can be racist	10%
Be open to valuing diversity	21%
Invest in the development of capacity	23%
Openness to change	30%

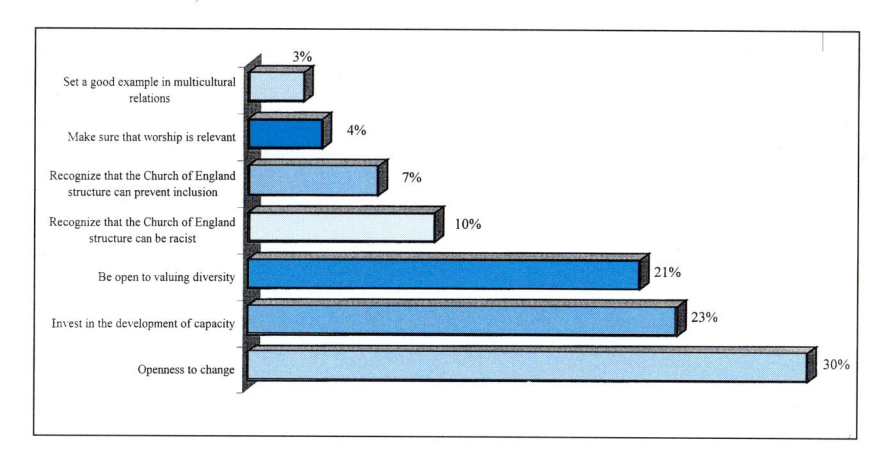

Figure 4.8 *Youth leaders' suggestions for issues that the Church of England needs to address*

ACTIVELY PROMOTE THE CHURCH AS AN EXAMPLE OF GOOD PRACTICE IN MULTICULTURAL RELATIONS

Forty-five per cent of the youth workers who participated in the discussions suggested that the Church should be the first one in setting an example of good practice in multicultural relations. Some of the comments included:

Research findings

> 'The Church needs to set good examples/provide role models.'
>
> 'The way the Church organizes itself, it needs to show quality and it needs to stay focused in what it's offering. In other words we can say it needs to market its product well.'
>
> 'I feel we as workers need to learn to say no to the pressures put on us by the church structures, in order to maintain quality.'

MAKE SURE WORSHIP AND OTHER CHURCH INITIATIVES ARE RELEVANT

A number of the youth workers felt that the Church needs to make its initiatives for young people from minority ethnic backgrounds relevant to their needs and also to different cultural experiences of Christianity. Comments included:

> 'Make worship fun and alive.'
>
> 'The way biblical teaching is approached can be inappropriate and consequently boring. Different cultures have different approaches to valuing Scripture . . . we should let the Bible speak for itself, . . . use the stories in the Bible more and find ways of making Bible studies relevant to the needs of young people from different cultures.'
>
> 'The Church of England needs to help young people to find answers to the questions they ask.'
>
> 'Help young people understand the importance and function of traditional services. Most of the time the young people do not really understand it and are put off from participating.'
>
> 'Mission trips for young people to practise their faith and to see it in practice.'

Develop Church structures that ensure the involvement of young people

All the youth leaders/workers felt that the Church needs to reshape its structures so that it includes and values young people and minority ethnic groups. Comments included:

> *'The Church of England will have to develop an openness to structural change.'*
>
> *'It needs to develop its own equality policy.'*
>
> *'Organize Youth Synods or forums, formally structured, where young people can meet and make decisions, and can influence the church.'*

Recognize that the existing Church of England structure can be racist

Some participants felt very strongly that it is important for the Church of England to recognize that its existing structure may be inappropriate for people from different minority ethnic groups and that it can be racist. Comments included:

> *'The Anglican Church's monolithic quality does not help.'*
>
> *'The Church of England needs to recognize that it is not moving with the community.'*
>
> *'The Church of England is reserved and culturally unaware.'*
>
> *'Recognize the fact that there is institutional racism within the Church.'*

Be open to valuing diversity

All the youth leaders felt that the Church needs to value the role of young people from minority ethnic backgrounds and demonstrate an openness to welcome other cultures with their diversity. One way of showing interest in other people's cultures is by learning about them. Some comment were as follows:

> 'The Church needs to become more welcoming, accepting and be aware of different cultures and their needs.'
>
> 'The Church itself needs to get back to the basics of loving people as they are.'
>
> 'Help people to feel valued and welcome. Help them know that their size and voices are valued.'
>
> 'Promote cultural awareness among the clergy.'
>
> 'The Church of England needs to recognize that when it was established its ways of working were not intended to reflect the cultural diversity that now exists in the Christian world. It is not reasonable to expect to include everyone. Therefore it should not expect the minority ethnic communities to do things its way. It cannot lump people together.'
>
> 'The Church needs to help people slowly build the transformation, become confident and comfortable in moving from being a single group towards integrating with the wider Church.'
>
> 'Encourage priests from other cultures to come and work with the Church of England.'

Discussions with representatives and groups of other faiths

In order to help gain an understanding of the degree to which the experience of Christians from minority ethnic communities is either similar to or different from that of young people of other faiths living in the United Kingdom, the survey was extended to include a Muslim group, a Hindu youth leader and a Sikh group.

MUSLIM YOUTH GROUP, MAIDENHEAD

Leaders at the Muslim Youth group saw their work with young people as an important and integral part of providing teaching about Islam. They also felt that it helped the young people to learn about their religious responsibilities and to become good citizens. They were also involved in organizing religious celebrations and summer camps. The camps were organized to help young people understand their theology as well as helping them deal with issues like bullying and racism. Additional help was given with information about training and employment opportunities.

A group of about 25 teenage boys took part in a discussion around the themes of the project. The group acknowledged that they experience problems both as a minority ethnic community and as individuals, but explained that in their view minorities do experience problems. The main issue raised by the group during the discussion was that they were proud of being Muslim whether their background was from Pakistan, India or Bangladesh. They felt it was their faith that determined their identity and not the country their parents had come from.

They also felt that their religion gave them guidance on all aspects of life and therefore it is the best way of life.

Discussion with representative of Vallabhnithi, a Hindu group in Ealing

The group places great emphasis on ensuring that young people are invited and included in all different aspects of the religious ceremonies and celebrations. Inclusion in worship through singing was considered to be an important part of the life of the community. The representative believed that parents played an important part as role models for their children and young people. They invite religious speakers from India to teach at whole community gatherings that include children and young people. Details of issues faced by young people were not included in the discussion.

Discussion with young people from Sikh faith, Slough

The group consisted of 11 young people and two leaders. The meeting took place at a Sikh Gurdwara (Temple) in Slough.

Key issues for the group were:
- A welcoming environment is essential and a great emphasis is placed on the creation of a community atmosphere in the temple. A complete meal is always provided for everyone who comes to the Gurdwara on Sundays.

Research findings

- People of all ages are involved in the life of the Gurdwara, worshipping, socializing, sharing in the preparation of food and in eating together.
- Young people are involved in serving, helping in the kitchen, making speeches, cleaning and looking after the shoes, etc. The Temple organizes other activities including summer camps for young people of different ages, sports and Punjabi language school.
- The motivation for the young people to attend, in addition to encouragement, was the variety of activities that surrounds involvement in worship; the group emphasized the positive feeling of participating in the process of worship in the Gurdwara: *'We like meeting family and friends, worship, serving, eating sweets, and dressing up in nice clothes.'*
- The young people clearly valued their identity as young Sikhs in the wider Sikh community. They were proud of being Sikh and felt comfortable in discussing their experience of faith with elders in the community.
- They also felt comfortable about relating to young people from other faiths. *'We have friends from other faiths, we respected them for being human beings rather than what they believed in.'*
- During the discussion about things which need to be addressed in relation to the needs of young people from minority ethnic backgrounds, the group raised the issue of the need for relevance in teaching. They felt it was essential for the parents and elders to make sure that whatever teaching they gave to young people did not contradict what they actually experienced in the community and that it was not undermined by the older people not doing what they said.
- They also emphasized the importance of young people being sure of their identity: *'Being confident helps us to be good people and helps us to relate to other young people around us. If you are not sure who you are you spend all the time either pretending or taking the wrong decisions.'*

Suggestions made by CMEAC diocesan network in response to the draft findings of the survey

As an integral part of the project, the researcher presented a summary of the draft report to the CMEAC Diocesan network meeting, followed by a discussion and workshop. The workshop looked at the issues raised by the research and involved participants in identification of issues which affect young Christians from minority ethnic communities. The following issues were identified:

NATIONAL LEVEL

- Identify the issues, allocate people to follow up and give deadlines.
- Develop an ethos and examples of good practice.
- Minority ethnic issues should be addressed in the context of theology, part and parcel of Christian doctrine.
- There are no 'real' Black people in position of authority.
- More Black history needs to be taught.
- Build up a collection of Black history.
- Education should be based on peer group 'models'.
- More role models are required within the community.
- It is not necessarily a good idea for White people to choose what is good for Black people.
- Openness to change is required.
- Be 'subtle'/gentle in the way we challenge/confront people about their racism or racist tendencies.
- The issue of Minority Ethnic Anglican Concerns should be on the agendas of the Board for Social Responsibility and the Council for Christian Unity.
- Get away from stereotyping.

Research findings

LOCAL LEVEL

- 'Free up' worship.
- Listen to young people.
- PCCs should include young people.
- Promote learning about minority ethnic communities.
- Develop supportive structure.
- Encourage individuals to talk about/demonstrate their own cultures.

Chapter 5

Examples of 'best practice'

During the project work examples of 'best practice' were identified, based on the guidelines for evidence-based practice in work with young people, as highlighted in the statement of purpose for the Youth Service agreed at the Ministerial Conference on the Youth Service (Huskin 1996).

The guidelines suggest that good youth work should be:

• **educative:** enabling young people to develop the skills, knowledge and attitudes needed to identify, advocate and pursue their rights and responsibilities as individuals and as members of groups and societies;

• **designed to promote equality of opportunity**: through challenging oppressions such as racism, sexism and all those which spring from differences of culture, race and language, sexual identity, gender, disability, age, religion and class, through the celebration of diversity and the strength that comes from those differences;

• **participatory**: through a voluntary relationship with young people in which young people are partners in a team processes and decision-making structures which affect their own and other young people's lives and environment;

• **empowering**: supporting young people in understanding and acting on the personal, social and political issues which affect their lives, the lives of others and the communities of which they are a part.

Examples of 'best practice'

1. Title/Work Area Act One, Diocese of Birmingham

Description of the initiative 'Act One' is a Christian residential week for young people from Urban Priority Areas in Birmingham. It is designed to help young people from different communities in their personal and spiritual development by encouraging them to participate in various innovative activities.

'Act One' also provides leadership training and development opportunities for young people.

Community groups involved in project Young people both male and female, aged between 12 and 16, from different cultural backgrounds.

Relationship to Church Supported by the diocese. The young people come from different churches in Birmingham.

Factors that are seen as significant in the success of the activity

- Young people feel valued, and that it is their time.
- An opportunity to identify and encourage talents that young people may have to offer, which otherwise go unnoticed.
- A space in which young people meet each other, learn new skills and explore new experiences in new environments. Activities include music, dance, arts, walking, sports, and events such as ballooning..
- Promotes involvement in outdoor pursuits.

Contact address

Diocesan Youth Officer, Church House, Harborne Park Rd, Harborne, Birmingham B17 0BH (Tel: 0121 704 1911)

2. Title/Work Area   **Youth Forum Catholic Association for Racial Justice, London**

Description of the initiative The Youth Forum is a new initiative started by the Catholic Association for Racial Justice. Youth Project in London. It runs a series of one-day sessions that enable groups from minority ethnic backgrounds to participate in a number of different activities, including discussions, presentations, role plays and reflection sessions. The aim of the project is to provide a forum for young Christians (age 16 to 25) from minority ethnic backgrounds and who are at sixth form or university level, to express their concerns as young Christians and to share their hopes and talents. The project also aims to provide support and encouragement in relation to their rights and responsibilities towards each other and towards the community at large.

Community groups involved in project Young people from minority ethnic backgrounds who are studying at sixth form or university level.

Relationship to Church The project is run by the Catholic Association for Racial Justice and works with Catholic churches and schools.

Factors that are seen as significant in the success of the activity

- Gives young people a chance to meet with other young people of their age and faith.
- Gives them a chance to express their feelings, ideas and experiences.
- It provides a forum for minority ethnic young Christians to explore and develop their talents and be responsible members of the community.

Contact address: The Youth Project Leader, Catholic Association for Racial Justice, 9 Henry Road, Manor House, London N4 2LH (Tel: 020 8802 8080)

Examples of 'best practice'

3. Title/Work Area — Black Forum, Diocese of Southwark, London

Description of the initiative The Black Forum was set up five years ago, as a direct responsibility of the Bishop's Council, to provide opportunities for the Black members of the Church in the Southwark Diocese to make their voices heard and express their views, in any matters of interest, concern or importance. It holds a series of annual events to share and celebrate their roles and skills with the wider Church community.

In 2000, as part of their fifth Black Forum, a whole day event, including a variety of programmes, was put together for the Black and Asian families, the clergy and young people from the churches in the diocese.

A visit to Zimbabwe was also arranged for the young people from the Southwark Diocese to meet the friend churches there. Now the young people are raising money to invite a group of young people from Zimbabwe to visit them here.

Community groups involved in project Black and Asian communities and the clergy from different parishes in the Diocese.

Relationship to Church The Black Forum in Southwark Diocese was set up five years ago, as a direct responsibility of the Bishop's Council.

Factors that are seen as significant in the success of the activity

- Black and Asian families from different churches have a forum to meet each other.

- Provides a forum for the minority ethnic communities and the young Christians in the diocese to voice their ideas, concerns and feelings on matters of interest and importance.

- The annual events encourage the communities to share and celebrate their roles and skills.

Contact address: Southwark Diocese, Race Relations Commission, St Michaels Church Hall, Trundle Street, London, SE1 1QT
(Tel: 020 7403 6758)

4. Title/Work Area — Aston Community Youth Project, Birmingham

Description of the initiative   The project was set up in 1989 by a group of local churches, with the aim of reflecting Christian love and Christian values in the wider community. Over the years the project has developed into a charity working with and for young people. Participants are mainly from minority ethnic backgrounds and between the ages of 16 and 25. Many of them are unemployed, marginalized, disadvantaged and potentially at risk of getting involved in criminal and antisocial activities due to their economic and social situations.

The project works with young people in the local communities to help them improve their quality of life, through valuing them, befriending them and encouraging them to explore and develop their talents and potential. The work with young people, as individuals and groups, involves outreach programmes, centre-based activities, sports, music, residential sessions, and introducing them to opportunities in education, training and employment.

The project has also produced a video about racism in the community.

Community groups involved in project   Young people from the Newtown and Aston areas of Birmingham who are unemployed, marginalized, disadvantaged and at risk.

Relationship to Church   The project now runs as a charity, working in close cooperation and partnership with different churches in the area and other organizations committed to youth work with the disadvantaged.

Factors that are seen as significant in the success of the activity

- Valuing young people as human beings.
- Providing opportunities for disadvantaged young people to explore and develop their own potential and talents.
- Providing support and advice on education, training and employment opportunities.

Examples of 'best practice'

Contact address: Outreach Worker, Aston Community Youth Project, Lichfield Road Methodist Church, Lichfield Road, Aston, Birmingham, B6 5SX (Tel: 0121 326301)

5. Title/Work Area — The Encounter Youth Exchange Project, Diocese of Chelmsford

Description of the initiative The Encounter Youth Exchange Programme was an initiative organized by the Chelmsford Diocesan Interfaith Advisor, for young people of Christian, Muslim and Jewish faiths to visit the Holy Land, meet young people there and experience the life of young people in Jerusalem. The group is now working towards hosting a group of young people from Jerusalem on a visit to England. It was a part of the bridge building initiative by the Diocese.

Community groups involved in project The project involved young people from different faiths, cultures and ethnic backgrounds living in the United Kingdom.

Relationship to Church Chelmsford Diocese helped raised the funds. It organized and supported the project.

Factors that are seen as significant in the success of the activity

- Positive commitment and practical work to break barriers and build bridges between different faiths and different communities.

Contact address: The UK Coordinator for Encounter Youth Exchange Project, Chelmsford Diocese (Guy Harlings), 53 New Street, Chelmsford CM1 1AT (Tel: 020 8471 1788)

6. Title/Work Area — Bourn Parish, Cambridge

Description of the initiative The parish, located in rural Cambridgeshire, maintained their links with the Church in Zaire over the years as a supporting parish. Recognizing the need to go beyond simple financial support and also the presence of Congolese Christian refugees in the United Kingdom, the parish decided to build on its links and develop a working partnership with the Congolese Christian refugees in London, to help them, through guidance and support, in settling and coping with being in a different environment. The parish also invited them to its church and community in order to learn and exchange experiences of being Christian in different communities.

Community groups involved in project This is an ongoing support partnership that Bourn Parish has developed with one of the Congolese refugee communities in London.

Factors that are seen as significant in the success of the activity

- Regardless of being a predominantly White parish, Bourn church used the links experience to reassess and develop its relationship with a minority ethnic Christian community.

- The parish has been active in developing an environment where Christians can learn from each other's different cultural experiences and celebrate the diversity.

- The ministers in both congregations have worked at developing a mutually supportive relationship. The relationship of respect and support between the ministers has opened up new possibilities of working together in the future.

- The young Congolese community values its contact with the parish over the years and the sense of inclusion it continues to receive from them.

Contact address: The Minister, Papworth Team Ministry, 6 The Drift, Elsworth, CB3 8JN (Tel: 01954 267199)

Examples of 'best practice'

7. Title/Work Area — Black Methodist Youth Conference, Methodist Church

Description of the initiative The Black Methodist Youth Conference is organized annually for young Christians from the Methodist Church in the UK. The aim of the conference is to enable young people from African, African-Caribbean and Asian backgrounds to come together and share common interests, experiences, concerns, needs, talents and gifts. Also to encourage and empower young Christians to work towards building a better church and society.

Community groups involved in project Black Methodist Christians from different minority ethnic backgrounds, representing different churches in the UK.

Relationship to Church The conference is a part of the work of the Methodist Church through its Racial Justice office.

Factors that are seen as significant in the success of the activity

- Provision of opportunity and support for young people from minority ethnic backgrounds to meet each other and share ideas, concerns, views and experiences.
- Provision of an opportunity to learn about and share their history, culture and identity.
- Encouragement to value and share their talents and gifts.
- Being recognized as an integral part of the Church.

Contact address: Connexional Secretary for Racial Justice, The Methodist Church, 25 Marylebone Road, London, NW1 5JR (Tel: 020 7486 5502)

8. Title/Work Area — **Asian Fellowship, Sheffield**

Description of the initiative The group has been set up to provide support for a relatively small number of South Asian Christians living in and around Sheffield. The group meets every month and young people are involved in playing music, singing, Bible reading, sharing and discussions.

The group is hosted by the local parish church which itself has a small, elderly and declining population that now lives in a Pakistani Muslim community. By working together the church has provided valuable support for the South Asian Christians who attend this church in helping them cope with the sense of isolation they often feel. But equally the South Asian Christians have brought new life to the church and helped it to overcome the threat of closure and also to meet the needs of their increasingly aging congregation.

Community groups involved in project Asian Christian families who attend different churches come together every month to worship and share ideas and experiences in their own language.

Relationship to Church The fellowship is hosted by the local parish church.

Factors that are seen as significant in the success of the activity

- Commitment to mutual involvement in shared learning, facilities and worship in order to meet differing needs.

Contact address: St Alban's House, 20 Chapelwood Road, Sheffield S9 5AY

Examples of 'best practice'

9. Title/Work Area — African and Caribbean Evangelical Alliance (ACEA), London

Description of the initiative African and Caribbean Evangelical Alliance's Children & Youth Commission has been established with the aim of facilitating the spiritual, social, physical, emotional and mental development of all children and young people in Black Majority Churches and the Black community in general.

Community groups involved in project Groups and individuals from the Black Majority Churches and the wider community in the UK.

Relationship to Church ACEA works in cooperation with the Black Majority Churches throughout the UK.

Factors that are seen as significant in the success of the activity

- Working together to run programmes:

Safe and Sound: Child Protection Conferences.

Faith in the Future: Youth programme, encouraging young people in their spiritual growth.

Empower: Training programme for youth workers.

Contact address: National Youth, Community Development and Training Officer, African and Caribbean Evangelical Alliance (ACEA), Whitefield House, 186 Kennington Park Road, London SE11 4BT (Tel: 020 7735 7373)

10. Title/Work Area — **Bible Club and Asian Christian Ministry, Oxford**

Description of the initiative The group is made up of young South Asian Christians, their parents and White English members of the Christian community. The group meets regularly for Bible study, singing, sharing of food and culture, as well as social events, fund raising and outings.

Community groups involved in project Asian and White English Christian community groups.

Relationship to Church The groups come from St Mary's Parish.

Factors that are seen as significant in the success of the activity

- Christians from different cultural backgrounds committed to trying to get to know each other, through sharing in worship, singing in each other's languages, sharing food and working together.
- Inclusion of Christians of different ages including young people creates an opportunity for the young and grown-up people to work together.

Contact address: Link Person, Parish of St Mary's, 94 Bayswater Road Headington, Oxford OX3 9NZ (Tel: 01865 452572)

Examples of 'best practice'

11. Title/Work Area   Timothy Fellowship, London

Description of the initiative The group is made up of young people from Chinese backgrounds who came to Britain in their youth and did not necessarily have their families here with them. They meet every Sunday for worship and meet as a youth group after the service. They are involved in planning, arranging discussions, Bible study and social activities. They work together as a support group for each other and feel that this opportunity of meeting provides them with a forum for getting together, sharing experiences and learning from each other as well as being able to share their mother tongue and same cultural values.

Community groups involved in project Young Christians from Chinese backgrounds, studying or working in and around London.

Relationship to Church The group is run and supported by the Chinese-speaking congregation at St Martin's in the Fields, London.

Factors that are seen as significant in the success of the activity

- A support forum, where young people are able to meet those who share the same language and culture.
- The group is involved as a team in planning, arranging and evaluating group activities together.

Contact address: The Youth Worker, Timothy Fellowship, c/o Chinese-Speaking Fellowship, St Martin's in the Fields, Trafalgar Square, London WC2N 4JJ   (Tel: 020 7925 0755)

Additional examples of agencies working for young people

Fury (Fellowship of United Reformed Youth) Assembly
United Reformed Church
86 Tavistock Place
London
WC1H 9RT

Tel: 020 7916 8682

Young Adult Network
The Coordinator
c/o The National Youth Office
Church House
Great Smith Street
London
SW1P 3NZ

Tel: 020 7898 1509

Mission to London
Youth Project Coordinator
Common Wealth Church
PO Box 15058
London
W11 3ZT

Tel: 020 7792 9913

CHAPTER 6

Recommendations

The following recommendations are based on the findings of the research work.

Develop a Church that has an ethos and structure which actively promotes inclusion and diversity.

A key theme raised at all stages of the research was the need for the Church of England to develop organizational structures which include and value young minority ethnic Anglicans. This could be addressed by adding structures onto the existing format of church organizations. However, consideration would need to be given as to whether or not this approach would meet the overwhelming demand for the development of inclusive approaches. As suggested by Phillips (1997), the problem is that the 'add on' approach offers a 'disturbingly frozen solution' where people stay isolated with no development of mutual understanding, and relationships remain 'fragile and grudging'. The Church will need to address the needs of young Christians from all cultures, by focusing on developing ways of valuing youth in all their cultural and social diversity as inherent elements of Christian identity.

Positive Action	Action by:
• The Church should explore and develop positive ways of working which unite its members by supporting diversity, and promoting opportunities for young people.	National, diocesan and parish bodies

- The Church of England needs to set out a national policy of inclusiveness, whereby all young people's gifts, including those of minority ethnic young people, are valued and used.

Archbishops' Council

Aim to be a 'role model'

English culture is one in which diversity of beliefs, social values and spiritual experience have traditionally been expressed by the creative development of church movements which do not conform to the Church of England's structures. From the comments made by participants it was clear that denominations were not important to some of the young people. Above all, they valued involvement in churches and groups which helped them to explore the challenges and opportunities which they face in life.

Within this context, perhaps the simplest approach to addressing the needs of young minority ethnic Anglicans is for the Church of England to focus on building good practice by actively promoting partnerships with other denominations, communities and faith groups, as well as marginalized and disadvantaged groups, in order to help young people develop their potential as human beings.

Positive Action

- Work should be undertaken to develop the skills of both lay and ordained people so that they can confidently address the fundamental responsibility that the Church has and to work with and for all its members, in all their richness and diversity.

National, diocesan and parish bodies

- The Church should intensify its efforts to actively challenge institutional racism by establishing programmes at diocesan and parish levels which develop and promote positive strategies towards valuing cultural diversity.

Diocesan and parish bodies

CMEAC

Recommendations

- Encourage partnerships between Christians from different denominations, and with other faith groups, in order to support and promote opportunities for young people. — **National, diocesan and parish bodies**

- Training in anti-racism and awareness of cultural diversity should be offered to youth officers/workers so that they will have the confidence and understanding needed to work with young people from minority ethnic communities. — **National and diocesan bodies**

- Provide training for ordained and lay Church workers in skills that give them confidence to work with young people from culturally diverse environments. This can be done by organizing and promoting a network of people with appropriate experience who are prepared to provide training. — **Diocesan and parish bodies**

- Support and encourage young adults to accept leadership roles, providing positive role models for others in the future. — **Parish clergy**

- Enable young minority ethnic Anglicans to fulfil their vocations as youth workers/Youth Officers, Church and community leaders. — **Diocesan Youth Officers, parish clergy and youth workers**

Encourage supportive links across all bodies

It was clear from the projects and groups visited during the research that successful work was built upon the strengths of individual churches, and also involved links and relationships which included a wide range of people from various denominations, cultures and communities. The success of any future work will depend heavily on the promotion of supportive networks for the exchange of ideas on youth programmes and worship.

Positive Action

- Develop the work begun during this research project of identifying, encouraging and networking with projects involved in work with young Anglicans from minority ethnic backgrounds, by exploring the possibility of establishing a central resource which can act as a catalyst for the development of a support network. **CMEAC**

- Appoint a full-time worker to implement an effective programme. **National bodies**

- Develop an action plan to encourage supportive links between Christians from a wide range of backgrounds, also to facilitate and promote the exchange of spiritual, social and cultural experiences. Develop strategies which encourage shared worship events, partnership in tackling social issues and community needs, joint outreach work, exchange programmes, shared involvement in arts, recreational and sports activities. **CMEAC**

- Organize local training in approaches to developing partnerships. **Dioceses and parishes**

Recommendations

- Promote information about initiatives at parish and national levels through the media, for example, Christian publications, parish magazines, websites. — **CMEAC parishes**

- Ensure that the resource and training materials developed for young people in the Church of England are representative of all communities. — **National, diocesan and parish bodies**

Stimulate a sense of self-worth in young Anglicans from all communities

Although limited, the work done with other faith groups showed the value of promoting of identity as an integral part of inclusion in the faith groups. While all faith groups have divisions, the impression given by the young people from both the Islamic and Sikh communities was of the importance of the faith group identity being valued over and above cultural or 'racial' identity. This contrasted strongly with the sense of confusion over identity expressed by many of the young Christians from minority ethnic communities involved in the survey.

In research work which explored experiences faced by young Asians living in the UK Paul Ghuman (1999) recognized that support for the development of clear identities was important for children from the Sikh, Muslim and Hindu faiths. The comments of the young Christians in the research indicated that they felt they had little support for the development of a positive self-identity as Christians as well as members of a community. It therefore seems important that any work undertaken by the Church to support young people must strongly emphasize the development of self-esteem.

Stimulate a sense of self-worth

- Develop inclusive structures within the Church which create an environment in which young Christians can learn skills and gain confidence in developing their social and spiritual potential. — **All bodies**

- Take an active role in promoting understanding of the social and spiritual qualities of Christians whose lives have been shaped by different cultures. — **CMEAC, BoEd, dioceses and parishes**

- Establish a forum at the national level which encourages young Christians from different community backgrounds to participate in the decision-making structures of the Church. — **CMEAC BoEd, Young Adult network**

- Organize a range of experiences at diocesan level in order to find effective ways of involving minority ethnic young people in the decision-making structures of the Church. — **Dioceses**

- Develop further the work of the Young Adult Network and the Young Synod Observer Group by encouraging minority ethnic Anglicans to participate.

Allocation of resources

Progressing beyond add-on approaches to meeting the needs of young Anglicans from different cultural backgrounds will require allocation of human and financial resources as integral elements of mainstream planning. Commitment to this needs to be owned and addressed at the very highest level of the Church. — **Archbishops' Council**

References

The General Synod Board of Education, *Youth A Part: Young People and the Church,* London: Church House Publishing, 1996.

Paul A. Singh Ghuman, *Asian Adolescents in the West,* London: British Psychological Society, 1999.

John Huskin, *Quality Work with Young People,* London: National Youth Agency, 1996.

Tariq Modood, *Church, State and Religious Minorities,* London: Policy Studies Institute, 1997.

Sir Herman Ouseley, *Young and Equal. A Standard of Racial Equality in Services Working with Young People,* London: Commission for Racial Equality, 1995.

A. Phillips, *Religion and Public Life: Church, State and Religious Minorities*, ed. T. Modood, London: Policy Studies Institute, 1997.

The Stephen Lawrence Inquiry: Report of an Inquiry by Sir William McPherson of Cluny, 2 vols, London: The Stationery Office, 1999.

Index

ACEA (African and Caribbean Evangelical Alliance) 4, 58, 61
Act One (Birmingham Diocese) 50
activities for young people 4, 22–4, 37–43
African and Caribbean Evangelical Alliance (ACEA) 6, 61
Archbishops' Council recommendations 66, 70
Asian Fellowship (Sheffield) 57
Asian women 19
Asian young people 28, 31–2

'best practice' 52–64
Bible Club and Asian Christian Ministry (Oxford) 62
Bible study groups 5, 6, 18, 22, 24, 40
Birmingham
  Act One 50
  Aston Community Youth Project 53–4
Black Anglican Celebration for the Decade of Evangelicalism 6–7, 78
Black Methodist Youth Conference 59
Board for Social Responsibility 51
Bourn Parish (Cambridge) 55

Cambridge, Bourn Parish 5, 58
Catholic Association for Racial Justice 51
Chelmsford, Encounter Youth Exchange Project 57
Chinese young people 28, 31, 39, 63
Church denominations 3, 21–2, 37, 66
Church leaders 29–30, 35
Church organization/structures 4, 17, 20–21, 35–8, 44, 46, 65–6, 70
Church workers, training for 67

CMEAC (Committee for Minority Ethic Anglican Concerns) 1–2, 7–12, 50–51, 68–70, 79
cultural backgrounds 3, 11, 13, 27–8, 31–2, 40, 43–7
cultural diversity 4–7, 43, 44, 65, 67
cultural identity 27–31, 32, 33, 34, 50, 69

discussion process 9–11, 30, 48–50

Encounter Youth Exchange Project (Chelmsford Diocese) 57
equal opportunities 20, 52

Fury (Fellowship of United Reformed Youth) Assembly 64

good practice 5, 51, 52, 63
group leaders/agencies *see* youth officers/workers/leaders
group work 19–20
groups 23–7

Hindus 5, 12, 35, 49, 69

inclusion 3, 4, 25, 29
institutional racism vii, 19, 33, 46

JOYNT HOPE 8, 10

Methodist Church, Black Methodist Youth Conference 59
methodology 8–11
Ministerial Conference on the Youth Service 52
Mission to London 64

Index

Muslims   5, 12, 34, 48, 69

Oxford, Bible Club and Asian Christian Ministry   62

parents   28, 31, 35–6, 50
projects identified by the respondents   18–19

research findings 12–48
role models   35, 45, 51, 66–7

services   4, 36–7, 45
sexism   52
Sheffield, Asian Fellowship   60
Sikhs   5, 12, 35, 49–50, 69
Southwark Diocese, Black Forum   52
survey methods   8–9

Timothy Fellowship (London)   63

United Reformed Church   64

Vallabhnithi (Hindu young people's group)   5, 12, 49, 69

women   17, 19
worship   5, 25, 26, 29, 39, 44, 45

Young Adult Network   64, 70
Young Synod Observer Group   70
youth clubs   22, 27, 30
Youth Forum Catholic Association for Racial Justice (London)   54
youth officers/workers/leaders   38–9, 40–3, 43–4
summary of work   4–5

Zaire, and Bourn Parish (Cambridge)   58
Zimbabwe, and the Southwark Diocese Black Forum   55